"If all economists were laid end to end, they would not reach a conclusion."

George Bernard Shaw

Experience in following economic and business headlines over the past three to five years would suggest that Mr. Shaw hit the nail right on the head. However, what economists do seem to agree upon is the fact that these past several years have been reflective of significant instability and uncertainty in the economic and job markets. In fact, as of today, the federal unemployment rate sits at 10.1%. Interestingly, even though corporate earnings in general appear to be on the rebound, and in spite of a significant influx of funding from the federal government, our unemployment rate continues to be relatively frozen at this painfully high level. One reason proposed for the slow improvement in the job situation is that companies are experiencing a great deal of uncertainty when looking at the horizon long term. This uncertainty appears to be resulting in a desire to protect cash reserves in anticipation of further economic instability in the near future. This has certainly been just one explanation offered for the limited job growth, and I realize that there are many other possible explanations. However, regardless of the reasons for the current situation, the fact remains that ten out of every one hundred able-bodied adults in this country are currently unemployed.

The current economic picture essentially has forced change to occur where change was not necessarily wanted or needed. This is true for both employers and employees. For employers, we have seen that they have been forced to reduce or streamline personnel, re-deploy personnel, leverage other assets, and otherwise engage in creative moves designed to preserve life and function enough to remain a viable entity. Unfortunately, what this means is that for many employees, there is a tremendous sense of uncertainty and instability, knowing that one's future employment status and security with a company may now be in jeopardy through no direct fault of their own.

"Everything is connected . . . no one thing can change by itself."

Paul Hawken, 1994

Be it desired or not, change is still change, and for many people, it represents further insecurity, instability, and discomfort. Walk into the business section of a bookstore, and you'll see the numerous books that have been published designed to help facilitate change within organizations. The mere number of authors and different perspectives on the subject provides evidence that, for most people, change is a difficult process. It becomes even more difficult when people perceive that change is being forced upon them against their will. However, if we conceptualize change from a systemic standpoint, it becomes fairly easy to help individuals begin to gain a greater sense of stability during these otherwise unstable and uncertain times.

According to Dictionary.com, a system is defined as an "orderly assemblage of facts, parts, etc., forming a whole." It is also defined as "the body as a whole functioning unit." A system is a collaborative integration of multiple, but separate, parts that work together to function as a whole. In order for systems to survive and to maintain functioning, it is necessary for all parts of the system to maintain a rather symbiotic relationship with all other parts of the system. For example, if we take a look at our current educational system, we can see that within that system are four primary parts: students, educators, administrators, and parents. In order for the educational system to work at its maximum potential, all four of these parts must be in a collaborative and symbiotic relationship. When parents and students are reading off the same page as educators and administrators are, we should expect to see higher performing academic output.

One characteristic of all systems, however, is a capacity for a certain degree of flexibility. In other words, all systems have the capacity to flex and then and stretch or constrict as needed in order to improve the overall integrity of the system. This is true for all systems, up to a certain point. Beyond this point, the system begins to disintegrate and no longer functions effectively. Again, referring back to our educational system example, we can see, for instance, when there is a decline in student enrollment, there has to be a compensatory decline in the number of educators or administrators in order to balance out the overall system. Likewise, if we see greater parental involvement in children's educational experiences, as is the case with paraprofessionals, we can also compensate for this within the system by decreasing the number of administrators or educators such that the entire educational system continues to maintain its adequate or better level of functioning while parts within the system fluctuate up or down. All systems, however, have a breaking point. While systems are made to flex and bend, there is a limit on the degree of flexing or bending they can do while maintaining integrity. For example, if an extraordinarily large number of parents desire roles as paraprofessionals in their students' classrooms, even though they may not have been adequately trained in childhood education, we likely will see a dramatic decrease in academic performance and effectiveness. If this trend continues, then it is likely that the educational system will begin to deteriorate and essentially fall apart.

So systems theory basically says the following: systems are made of parts, these parts must work together in order to maintain functioning of the system, the individual parts have room to change and adapt in response to changes in other parts of the system up to a certain point, and changes in one aspect of the system that are either too extreme or that are not adequately compensated for by other parts of the system will result in a deterioration and breakdown of systemic functioning. It is in this systems model of looking at things that people can begin to regain a sense of security and stability when so many things going on around them seem to be unstable. We are parts of a larger system. While we may not be able to change the system itself, we can change our response to the system and adapt our piece of the system in order to facilitate more comfort, effectiveness, and control.

"Economists are about as useful as astrologers in predicting the future (and, like astrologers, they never let failure on one occasion diminish certitude on the next)."

Arthur M. Schlesinger, Jr., 1993

Generally speaking, the changes we have seen in our economy and in our overall employment outlook represent a destabilization within our social economic system. In other words, the healthy functioning of our economy depends on collaboration between the parts of this system—namely private-sector employers, federal employers, legislative influences, global influences, and of course individual employees. We have seen significant changes in each of the above parts of the economic system over the past several years, with perhaps the only exception being that of individual employees. For the most part, we have not seen a significant change in people's desire to attain and maintain consistent gainful employment. However, we have seen significant changes in the other aspects of the economic system that have directly affected individual employees' ability to work in the capacity they prefer. So we see the changes in these parts of the economic system represent a destabilization in the overall system's functioning. Now the good news is that all systems eventually re-stabilize. The better news is that there are ways to have some control over how systems re-stabilize. More specifically, there are ways individual employees can gain some degree of control over their own functioning and effectiveness within the larger economic system that, in turn, will hopefully increase the health of the individual part of the system (i.e., individual employees) while eventually also positively influencing other factors within the greater economic system.

According to research produced by the <u>Conference Board</u> in February of 2008, only 55% of American workers who were earning more than fifty thousand dollars per year reported being satisfied with their jobs at the time. Only 14% of these people claimed that they were "very satisfied." Further, the same study revealed that 25% of employees are simply "showing up to collect a paycheck." The interesting thing about this research is that it was conducted in 2005, before much of the current economic instability began to be seen. In other words, even when economic conditions appear to be relatively stable, a large percentage of American workers appear to be significantly dissatisfied in their current employment setting. Given the state of economic affairs in 2010, there is no reason to think that employees suddenly became more satisfied in their jobs. More likely, dissatisfaction has increased as instability and insecurity have increased.

As stated earlier, the current employment picture is not a pretty one. As of July of this year, 8.68 million people between the ages of twenty-five and fifty-four years were unemployed. Of these, 2.69 million are classified in the "management, professional, business, and financial operations" sectors. Additionally, as of December of last year, 2.1 million of these unemployed had college degrees or better. These statistics, as provided by the US Bureau of Labor Statistics, are significant not only because of the fact that so many people are unemployed, but also because of the fact that so many folks who are well educated are also finding themselves being displaced during these difficult economic times. Historically, we have seen that jobs in the manufacturing and retail sectors are usually the first to go in difficult economies, but today, we're seeing folks from all industries and at all educational levels being impacted by our current economic conditions.

Based on current statistics as well as research from employment satisfaction studies prior to the economic downturn, it is easy to imagine what those who remain employed may be feeling. If only 55% were satisfied with their current jobs during what could be described as calm and stable economic conditions, it is hard to believe that they would be any more likely to be satisfied in their work during these current unstable and unpredictable economic conditions. Additionally, those who remain employed are likely to be experiencing a greater degree of insecurity, feeling that their future employment status is dependent on people or factors that lie outside of their control.

The goal of this book is to provide information that will allow individuals, both employed and unemployed, to gain a greater sense of control and stability during these unstable economic conditions. As Stephen Covey is known for espousing, the most highly effective people are able to identify those things that are in their control and act on those things while letting go of things that are outside of their control. To some degree, this is our goal for today. When individuals feel that they have control over themselves, their decisions, and their futures, they gain an inherent sense of security and stability. This serves as a tremendous buffer against periods of instability or other external inconsistencies that may be going on around them.

This book is designed primarily for those who've been recently displaced from employment, those who are currently dissatisfied in their chosen career path, as well as those who are ready to start thinking about their encore career. This book is also likely to be useful for those who enjoy what they're doing but who simply want to make themselves more relevant within their own organization. In other words, essentially, the material here is relevant for any of those individuals who want to regain some degree of control over their professional lives, anybody who wants to find satisfaction in his or her career, as well as folks who are ready to move on to something new and different. It's all designed to help individuals gain a sense of security and stability in times of uncertainty and instability.

> "It seems to me . . . that external circumstances often serve as occasions for a new attitude to life and the world, long prepared in the unconscious, to become manifest."
>
> *Carl G. Jung*

In my work, both with clients who have been displaced as well as clients who remain employed but fear that their employment is tenuous, I have noticed that the one thing they share in common is a perception that they are in crisis. Namely, those who are out of work feel like they have become unemployed due to no fault of their own, while many of those who remain employed have very little trust or confidence that they, too, will not soon be displaced. Both report feeling a sense of powerlessness and loss of control that brings with it significant ambiguity over the future. When such ingredients combine, it is easy for people to lose perspective.

There's an anonymous quote that says, "The crisis delivers or destroys according to the response it engenders." Likewise, Sir Francis Bacon was quoted as saying, "A wise man will make more opportunities than he finds." What we choose to see in life is often a reflection of what we look at. While it is easy for clients to feel that they are in crisis and have no control primarily because of the chaos and unpredictability around them, what they fail to see is that this may be the very best time to spend their energy seeking clarity and focus within themselves. In other words, clients need to recognize that although they may have very little control over larger economic conditions around them, *they do have a significant amount of control over their responses* to these economic conditions. Specifically, when clients realize that their energy may be best spent trying to identify ways to best position themselves for success when the economic system re-stabilizes, they automatically gain a sense of empowerment, security, and control. This is the goal in crisis situations, after all: identify the problem, focus on aspects of the problem within your control, and take action.

With proper perspective, clients can see the current economic climate as an opportunity rather than a crisis. Namely, this becomes an opportunity to reevaluate a current career focus and to take this chance to redesign that career path in order to prepare and be excited about moving back into the market in a "better fit" career when the economy eventually recovers. In other words, the economy will eventually recover, and jobs will eventually return. So this being said, now seems to be the best time to take steps to return to a job you love rather than one you're simply familiar with but may not be fully satisfied with.

Okay, so perhaps I've convinced you that now would be a good time to reevaluate your career path in order to better find what may be your "ideal career." Nothing is perfect in life, and so there is no reason to think that there is a perfect career out there for any of us. However, we can aspire to have a greater degree of satisfaction in our chosen career path than what the statistics seem to say most of us actually experience. Career satisfaction is an important part of overall health and wellness of individuals, but there is research to show that there is also an organizational benefit when employees and careers have a better fit, meaning when employees are more aligned with the careers they've chosen.

In research conducted by Missouri State University assistant professor of management Wesley Scoggins, he cites a study conducted by the consulting firm Towers Perrin, which found that the more meaning employees found in their work, the more satisfied they reported being in their work. This may not be a big surprise, but the same study also found that the more meaning employees found in their work, the greater benefit the same employees were to their organizations. That is, they were more productive. Now research is somewhat mixed as to the actual increase in productivity from employees who are more satisfied in the work; however, it is intuitive that greater worker satisfaction is certainly not a detriment to productivity. Therefore, greater career satisfaction means greater meaning, which, in turn, benefits both the employee and ultimately the organization.

We've all heard the saying, "Do what you love and you'll never work a day in your life." While some may think this is a Pollyanna-ish way of thinking, finding meaning in one's work is not necessarily reserved for "the lucky few." However, in order to find that meaning, you have to take a rather strategic approach towards career exploration. Oftentimes, people end up on a particular career path because of parental pressures and expectations, because of intellectual interests in college, or simply because of the opportunities that were presented to them when they were ready to go to work. Of course, this is an abbreviated list of reasons, but the point is that very few adults have actually decided to be strategic in choosing their career paths. The winning strategy for finding meaning in one's work is grounded in a solid self-assessment of personality traits, interests, skills, and values. When we fully explore these factors, we develop a clear understanding of ourselves. With this understanding, you can then narrow down the hundreds of different career fields and have a better chance of actually choosing one that is the best fit for you. It is this "best fit" concept that generated the above-mentioned research on meaningfulness and work. The research shows that those who rate their careers as being a "best fit" for their personalities, interests, and values also describe feeling more meaning in their work. So to find meaning in work, first come to a clear understanding of yourself, and then try to map the data onto a specific career field. Your odds of finding meaning at work will significantly increase if you do this. So how can you go about being purposeful and intentional when making your career choice?

The late Russian author Maxim Gorky once said, "When work is a pleasure, life is a joy. When work is a duty, life is slavery." These are profound words, indeed, but they do not provide any insight into how to obtain pleasurable work. After all, if work were all-pleasurable, would it still be called "work?" Even if work cannot be all fun, most of us would like to have a career that we derive pleasure and a sense of purpose from. And yet depending on the research you read, anywhere from 40 to 60% of the American workforce is less than satisfied with their current job. Clearly, finding satisfying work is not as easy as it may seem.

The research has already been cited about the relationship between increased satisfaction and meaning in one's work relative to the degree of "fit" there appears to be between an individual's personality, values, and interests relative to a chosen career path. So naturally, it would seem wise to choose a career path that has the highest degree of overlap among those three things. What many people do is look at various career options and then try to map them onto their personal characteristics. The problem with this approach is that an individual who starts by looking at the various occupations that may provide meaning, pleasure, and satisfaction is essentially looking for the proverbial needle in a haystack. Based on the pure number of jobs and career paths that are available, the odds of actually being able to find an ideal match seem stacked against you. According to the 2010 standard occupational classification system established by the <u>Bureau of Labor Statistics</u>, eight hundred and forty different jobs have been classified, contained within ninety-seven "minor" groups and twenty-seven "major" groups. Elsewhere in their database, the same Bureau of Labor Statistics has classified one thousand twenty-two different occupations. The US Department of Labor has coordinated another database, the occupational information network, which classifies nine hundred and sixty-five different occupations. It seems that the exact number of occupations available is yet to be firmly agreed upon, but it does seem clear that the options are many.

Based on the huge number of career options available, it would seem that a more efficient approach to finding an ideal career path would be to start first with an increased understanding of yourself. Namely, the more thoroughly you understand your primary personality traits and characteristics, interests, and primary values, the easier it then becomes to weed out many of the career paths that are catalogued in so many different databases.

"This is self-knowledge – for a man to know what he knows, and what he does not know."

Socrates

In my work as a psychologist, just about the first step in any client interaction is that of assessment. This assessment can take many forms and can be focused on many different areas, but the overall purpose and function of assessment is to help me efficiently and accurately get a clear picture of what may be going on with a client. How did he or she get where he or she is today? What does the world look like from where he or she is standing? And how far is he or she today from where he or she would like to be tomorrow, next month, next year, and so on? Having a clear understanding of where you are at any given moment is the best way to begin any process that involves moving away from where you currently are at any given moment.

When trying to regain a sense of control and security relative to your employment opportunities in a downward economic cycle, assessment again becomes the best place to begin. Too many times, people enter into a career field only to find out later that either the career did not live up to their expectations or they thought the career would be a better fit for them than it was. I spoke with a client recently who is in his third career, after trying two other very different careers first. There is absolutely nothing wrong with the "trial and error" approach to finding the ideal career, and this is typically how most of us find our career paths. However, it simply is not the most efficient strategy, and it certainly reduces the amount of control and/or predictability you have over the whole employment/career situation. Reducing control and predictability in unstable times will only add to your stress and worry rather than empower you.

When it comes to career planning and good self-assessments, there are two obvious areas that need to be explored and understood as deeply as possible. These two areas are where most career assessments, career counselors, and career coaches will focus their attention. The first area that gets the most attention from career counselors is that of interests. Beginning as early as middle and high school, counselors begin asking you to think about things that interest you. You can hear the conversation now.

> **Johnnie** (*a high school junior*) *to* **Ms. Smith** (*his*
> *counselor*)*:* "Ms. Smith, I'm not sure what I want to
> do when I grow up. Can you help?"
> **Ms. Smith***:* "Well, Johnnie, what do you like to do?"
> **Johnnie***:* "Gosh, I like to do lots of things."
> **Ms. Smith***:* "Like what?"
> **Johnnie***:* "I don't know . . . lots of things."

This conversation will then go back and forth for a while as the counselor grows more and more frustrated trying to help Johnnie narrow down all the many things he enjoys doing from one day to the next in a way that will help him focus on a future career field. Without an assessment of interests, this will wind up being a frustrating process for both of them, and the information it provides will be useless. A formal assessment of interests is needed in order to help people identify those things they are interested in, enjoy doing, or think they would enjoy doing. This is pretty straightforward. However, the value of doing a formal assessment for these interests is that it provides a structured process for folks to better clarify and articulate their interests. This, in turn, allows for easier integration and provides a summary that people can easily package and take with them moving forward. In other words, a formal interest assessment is a way for people to take a large, amorphous, sometimes overwhelming task and convert it to something that has structure, form, shape, and utility for them going forward. It's the difference between asking somebody what foods they like to eat versus walking with somebody through a grocery store and helping them shop more efficiently for their groceries as they learn how to plan for meal preparation.

After interests, the next most common assessment used by career counselors in their efforts to help clients identify a truer "fit" with a possible career is that of personality. A personality assessment, as part of a good career-planning package, is almost considered to represent good "standard of care." Personality is defined as a relatively durable constellation of characteristics and traits. The words "relatively durable" are significant in this definition. None of us behaves in the same way all the time under all circumstances. However, there are characteristics that we tend to display more times than not and in more situations than not. These outward displays of temperament and characteristics are collectively considered to represent our personality. One's personality is influenced by a combination of both genetic makeup as well as social and environmental influences. From birth, we display certain characteristics that are more biologically based. In other words, these characteristics are more likely to be directly attributable to genetic material given to us by our parents. Examples of temperament can be seen when we compare infants to one another. We look at one infant and say that the infant is overly fussy or seems to be easily frustrated while another infant seems constantly happy and almost impervious to frustration. As we continue to grow and experience the world around us, these basic temperamental displays become influenced by our societal, environmental, and learned experiences. By the time we grow into early adolescence (and certainly into adulthood), what started off as a baby who was perhaps easily frustrated now becomes an adult whom others would describe as easily distractible, quick to lose focus, easily discouraged, and so on. Thus, as with most aspects of human behavior, there is a distinct relationship between biology and our environment, and this interaction is collectively referred to as our personality. Our personalities are highly complex and highly sophisticated, and it is not possible nor is it necessary for us to intimately know every aspect of our personality. However, it does become quite useful and effective (and is a good indicator of overall psychological health) if we have an awareness and appreciation of our most salient personality characteristics and traits. The more we can come to understand how we behave and respond to internal and external experiences around us, the easier it is for us to structure our environment in such a way that is accommodating and pleasing to those characteristics. This is true of relationships and hobbies, and it is certainly true of our work. Career opportunities that involve duties and responsibilities that are consistent with one's most salient personality characteristics are most likely to be described as satisfying career paths by those who have chosen to pursue them.

When it comes to career counseling and career assessment, the more generic and sublime assessments will frequently stop with just an assessment of interest and personality. As noted earlier, these two are common assessments, and the combination of the two is considered an appropriate standard of care. However, research and experience has shown me that while these two assessments may be the standard, they certainly are not sufficient, and more information is still needed in order to help folks more effectively identify a career path that will lead to greater satisfaction and contentment for them. The piece that is often omitted in standard career assessments is the whole discussion and examination of one's basic values.

In school, and certainly in any religious studies, we are often taught the importance of values. However, it seems that once we get into adulthood, there appears to be very little discussion or interest in discussing values until one perceives that their values have been violated.

From a career-counseling standpoint, when we assess values, we're really trying to assess those concepts, situations, circumstances, or experiences that individuals find to be of great worth or importance. Essentially, what we're looking for is to help individuals identify what really motivates them from one day to the next. What are the things that really drive an individual day in and day out? These are the things that we consider to be values. Above, we discussed briefly the benefit of assessing one's interests and salient personality characteristics when trying to determine a career path. However, not only would it seem counterintuitive, but it would also seem totally shortsighted to not include in any career guidance discussion an assessment and debriefing of an individual's values. Values represent those things that people hold important, and while we can relatively easily align people with careers that match their interests and their personalities, when we incorporate their value systems into the decision matrix, the alignment process becomes much more complex. This is possibly why most assessments don't include a values component. However, we believe that without this values assessment, we may be short-changing clients in the long run. For if we align clients with a career path that matches their interests and their basic personality characteristics but does not honor the things that they value or the things that motivate them from one day to the next, we are ultimately doing them a disservice, and they are less likely to feel content in their chosen career path.

"The whole is greater than the sum of its parts."

Aristotle

I'm sure you're familiar with the saying, "The whole is greater than the sum of its parts." This quotation refers to a kind of synergy that develops in nonlinear systems such that the product of a collaboration and integration of different parts within the system produces more than a simple aggregate of the parts that would be found in a more linear system. An effective and high-quality career assessment package should represent the synergistic output of information that is more than a simple combination of three different assessments. We have created a product that we feel matches the gold standard of career counseling and guidance and produces such a synergistic output of information for clients who use it. This product is known as the VIP solution: V for values, I for interests, and P for personality.

The VIP solution is a web-based, scientifically validated combination of assessments that looks at one's primary values, expressed interests, and most salient personality characteristics. However, the VIP solution goes further than simply assessing these things. These three different assessments are then consolidated and mapped onto one another in such a way as to then map those results onto the variety of career options that are available. If clients have a firm understanding of their most salient personality characteristics, those things that motivate them the most from one day to the next, and those things in which they feel most interested, we can then begin to identify an ideal career path simply through the process of elimination. After all, there are only going to be so many different career paths that match one's interests, values, and personality characteristics. We feel the combination of the individual assessments, the reports generated from these assessments, and the integration and debriefing of these assessments by licensed psychologists is the "value-added" piece to the VIP solution. It is what separates the VIP Solution from most other career assessments on the market. What follows is a more detailed description of the VIP Solution.

Values

The VIP Solution utilizes the Motives, Values, Preferences Inventory™ (MVPI) constructed by Dr. Robert Hogan of Hogan Assessment

Systems (www.hoganassessments.com). It reveals a person's core values and key drivers (areas that motivate and energize an individual). This invaluable information is used for determining the kinds of environments in which a person will perform best. People's values influence their choices of jobs and careers. People like others who share their values and prefer to work in jobs that support their values. Organizations can use this information to ensure that a new hire's values are consistent with those of the organization. The Motives, Values, Preferences Inventory™ can also help identify areas of compatibility and conflict among team members as well as an organization's mission.

Interests

Keeping consistent with using the most scientifically validated and purpose-driven assessments, the VIP Solution incorporates one of the world's most widely used and respected career interest inventories, the Strong Interest Inventory® (Strong) (www.cpp.com). This inventory helps people identify careers to which they are most inherently drawn. For nearly eighty years, the Strong Interest Inventory® has provided time-tested, research-validated insights to help individuals in their search for a rich and fulfilling career. The Strong is modeled on Dr. John Holland's theory, which states that most people can be loosely categorized with respect to six types: Realistic, Investigative, Artistic, Social, Enterprising, and Conventional. Occupations and work environments can also be classified by the same categories. People who choose careers that match their own types are most likely to be both satisfied and successful. The Strong report can help you to understand more about yourself and how your individual skills and interests are related to your career choice.

Personality

The VIP Solution utilizes the 16PF® (5th Edition) (www.ipat.com) to scientifically assess work-oriented personality traits. The Career Development Report (16PF) can help you to understand more about yourself and how your unique personality strengths function to enhance career success. This assessment and the accompanying report identify work-related personality traits, including strengths and areas needing development. It is founded on thirty-five years of research and consulting and predicts career activity as well as career field and occupational interest scores. It is often used in career counseling to assess career direction in career validation, both for individuals and organizations.

So an ideal career assessment includes a close and thorough examination of at least three different domains: one's values, one's interests, and one's most salient personality characteristics. The VIP solution, in conjunction with the thorough integration and debriefing by licensed psychologists, offers clients an ideal career assessment package that meets and exceeds the standard of care for career counseling and provides a value-added service that we feel is rather unique within the career-counseling field. As part of the debriefing process of these assessments, a licensed psychologist will guide clients through the navigation and decision-making process in regards to identifying what they feel may be an ideal career path for them. In some cases, this can be a relatively quick process; for others, this could require extended homework on the part of the client. What follows in the Appendix is a very brief workbook that we offer clients who feel that they want to further delve into the assessment data as they attempt to map their ideal career path on their own. After the initial debriefing of the assessments, clients are well equipped to take that data and wrestle with as much or as little as they feel the need to. Of course, ongoing career coaching from our psychologists is available to clients, but sometimes they would rather navigate this process on their own. This is totally acceptable, as we are all different and we all need to be able to honor our own decision-making processes when undertaking such a significant venture. The following pages represent a workbook that may be useful for these clients and are shared with you today so that you might have a better understanding of what these assessments provide as well as how they can be useful in helping you identify your ideal career path.

This manuscript originally discussed how individuals can regain a sense of control in these difficult economic times that many find to be so uncertain and unstable. If you recall from earlier in the reading, predictability and control are two of the biggest buffers against stress that have been shown in the research. The VIP Solution offers users a significant amount of information about themselves, which they can then use to make their career search more efficient and hopefully more effective. When individuals feel that they are more empowered, more effective, and less confined or restrained by external factors, they are more likely to report feeling secure and stable. This is partially the purpose of the VIP Solution: to provide a way for folks to gain a sense of calm, control, and stability during these otherwise unstable and uncertain economic times. The use of scientifically validated information to help us guide and direct our life choices is the most effective way that we can navigate the turbulent waters of whatever is going on around us from one day to the next.

I thank you for taking the time to read through this manuscript and certainly wish you the very best in your career search. If there is anything we can do to be helpful to you in this process or if you would like more information on the VIP solution, I encourage you to access our website at www.VIPtransition.com. If you would like more information on the individual assessments used in the VIP Solution, I encourage you to go to each assessment publisher's website.

APPENDIX

VIP Solution Workbook

"The Whole is Greater Than the Sum of its Parts"

Aristotle

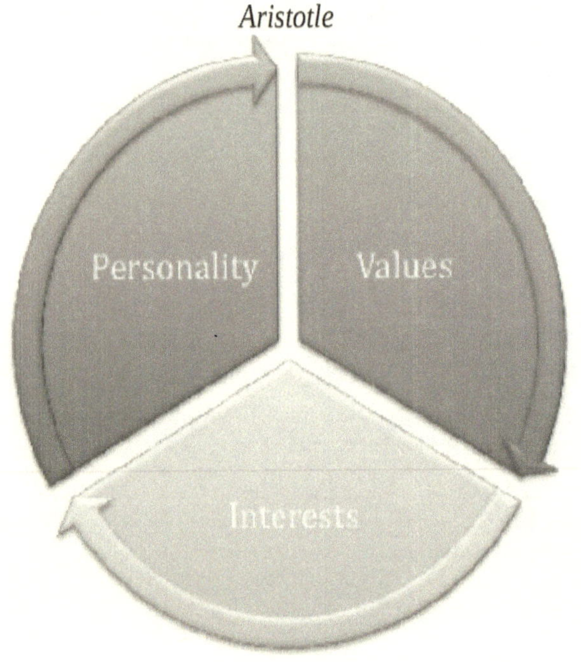

VALUES

According to Webster's Dictionary, values represent "a person's principles or standards of behavior; one's judgment of what is important in life." In theory, when we are thinking, acting, and feeling in ways that are consistent with our values, we are most likely to feel satisfied, content, and happy. This is true in relationships, in careers, and in life in general. Unfortunately, due to a variety of external and internal factors, we do not always honor our values on a consistent basis, and as a result, we may find ourselves feeling unsatisfied and frustrated. Therefore, during the pursuit of your future career, you would be best served by starting with a clarification of what you feel to be most important to you at this point in your life. This is the purpose of this section of the workbook and draws on information generated by the Motives, Values, Preference Inventory™. Please be thoughtful in your responses to the following questions.

From the MVPI™ report, what are your three main "Drivers," and what are some of the descriptors given for each?

DRIVER #1 -

Descriptors used for this driver include:

DRIVER #2 -

Descriptors used for this driver include:

DRIVER #3 -

Descriptors used for this driver include:

If one path to fulfillment is that of honoring your values, then this path can be met through honoring your values either in your professional life, your personal life, or some combination of the two. The more you are able to honor your values in your personal life, the less you will need to rely on honoring them in your professional life in order to feel an overall sense of satisfaction. Take a moment now and think about the following questions.

For each "Driver," to what extent and how is it being honored in your personal life?

DRIVER #1 -

DRIVER #2 -

DRIVER #3 -

For most who have been in a single profession or position for any length of time, at least some of our basic values are being honored to some degree. It is worth making note of which of those values are currently being honored in your current job in order to replicate them in your next pursuit and supplement what may be missing.

For each "Driver," to what extent and how is it being honored in your current professional life?

DRIVER #1 -

DRIVER #2 -

DRIVER #3 -

INTERESTS

It is almost intuitive, but when we are actively engaged in tasks or activities that interest us, we are more likely to feel satisfied in those tasks and are more likely to perform at a higher level. By taking a survey of your interests related to work, education, leisure activities, and so on, you can begin to bring your next career pursuit into clearer focus. Ideally, there will be an overlap between the things we think would be interesting and the things we feel we value. This is what you will be looking for as you thoughtfully respond to the following questions related to your interests. Information contained in the Strong Interest Inventory® Interpretive Report will be referenced for this section.

What is your 3-letter code (from page 2 of your report)?

How do the "representative interests" of each theme (as described on page 2 of your report) correlate with your expressed "Drivers" from the MVPI™ report (i.e., how do your interests overlap with your values)?

Narrowing the focus even further, what are your top three interest areas (from page 3 of your report)?

1. *Interest Area #1 is*
2. *Interest Area #2 is*
3. *Interest Area #3 is*

Within each of these specific interest areas, what are some of the aspects that are closely aligned with your "Drivers?"
Interest Area #1 -
Interest Area #2 -
Interest Area #3 -

PERSONALITY

This personality assessment summarizes how you are most likely to behave in normal, day-to-day situations. Unlike the first two assessments—in which you were asked about what you wanted, preferred, or liked—this assessment tells you what you are actually likely to see in yourself from one day to the next. Thus, independent of what we want or prefer, if our personality does not support this, we likely will not follow through with it. After thoroughly reading through your 16PF® Career Development Report, please respond thoughtfully to the following questions.

Looking at only the scales in which your score falls from 1-3 or from 8-10, please write down the basic descriptors that apply:

Which descriptors seem the most significant for you or seem to resonate most with you?

How can you see these descriptors being expressed in your current work setting in ways that are a "fit" between you and your career?

How can you see these descriptors being expressed in your current work setting in ways that are NOT a "fit" between you and your career?

In order to begin to map these results onto future possible career options, you need to again refer back to your values. From your MVPI™ report, examine whether any conflict exists between your primary "drivers" and your most salient personality characteristics. If so, then you will need to resolve that conflict before moving forward in your career decision. If no conflict exists, then refer to your interests and again assess for any conflicts that may exist.

CAREER MAPPING

At this point, you should have a clear understanding of your primary motivators, your expressed interests, and your most salient personality characteristics. You now have the essential data you need to begin mapping what should be an ideal career path. This can be the most frustrating and overwhelming part for people and is often why career coaching may be the best route to take. However, you are encouraged to attempt to navigate this process on your own first in order to see how far you can get.

The career mapping will require access to the Internet in order to access one major career website: the O*Net Resource Center, a federally funded and maintained occupational database.

Once on this website, use the "Find Occupations" tab to begin narrowing your career options. Click on the "Browse by O*Net Descriptor" tab and select the "Work Values" option. Referring back to your MVPI™ report, select the corresponding values on the O*Net site and begin looking at

possible job fields that may be a match for you according to your educational
level (or the level you are willing to complete).

**Make a list of the top ten jobs or job fields from the "Work
Values" list of O*Net's website that appear to be a strong
interest for you.**

**Now, do the same thing as above, only this time, choose the
"Interests" option under the "Browse by O*Net
Descriptor" tab. As with the values, select the appropriate
option for the interests as represented in your Strong
Interest Inventory® Report. Again, make a list of the top
ten jobs or job fields that appear to be a strong interest for
you.**

**Compare the two lists that you just created and search for
any overlap between the two. Are there any jobs, job fields,
or very similar job fields that are included on both lists? If
so, write these down here.**

From this point forward, you will need to commit to doing some
homework about each of the jobs or job fields listed in number three above.
Your homework will focus on learning as much as you can about the job, as
it really works from the inside out, and then assessing to what degree your
personality will or will not be a fit. This homework will include research on
the O*Net website, but it will also include any other readings you can do,
interviewing those who are already in the fire, and even possibly job
shadowing or serving an apprenticeship under those who may already be in
the field. The goal is to learn as much about the career as possible, including
the basic tasks and responsibilities of the career, the lifestyle afforded and
influenced by the career, the opportunities for growth and advancement in the
career, and so on. After this extensive homework, you should be in an ideal
position to confidently identify a career path that is more likely to be
consistent with your values, interests, and personality, thus leading to greater
contentment and satisfaction in your career path.